"Hope is not a matter of age"

A biography of Abbé Pierre - The French Priest

Paul V. Payton

Table of contents

Preview

Abbe Pierre was a humanitarian noted for his work with the destitute and was often chosen as France's most popular man.

He was born in Lyon, France, on August 5, 1912, into a wealthy and devoted Catholic family. Henri Grouès was given that name at birth. Inspired to lead a pious life from an early age, he joined the Capuchin monks in 1930. He remained for eight years, but suffered from the strict and austere lifestyle, in part because of his poor health.

As a result, he relocated to Grenoble and became a priest. He joined the resistance in 1942 and assisted in protecting local Jews from the Vichy police and the Nazis. He was eventually detained, but he was able to flee and join Charles de Gaulle's Free French after making his way to North Africa.

Abbe Pierre was elected to the French National Assembly after the war, although he believed he made little progress.

As a result, he decided to go and establish Emmanus in 1949. His charitable organization worked to provide refuge for the needy. However, he had a disdainful attitude toward the conventional understanding of generosity.

He believed that helping people assist themselves was the most effective kind of philanthropy. He believed that if charity were just a sarcastic gift given by the wealthy to the poor, it would serve no purpose other than to assuage the conscience of the wealthy.

Giving people a bed and a cause to leave is the company's attitude, according to the Emmanus branch on a British basis.

His charity also had a left-wing reputation since he believed that the money for it should come from wealthy people's surpluses that weren't required. After receiving political criticism, he said, "Knew nothing of left and right; the only extreme I support is upwards towards heaven."

He gave a passionate radio address in support of the homeless in 1954. His remarks struck a nerve with the French people when he said:

"My friends, lend a hand!" A lady who was holding the papers by which she was evicted from her house the day before recently died of exposure at three in the morning on the Boulevard Sebastopol.

Abbe Pierre rose to prominence as the unofficial homeless spokesperson. He was praised by a wide range of media and seemed to transcend the nation's political and religious divisions.

Catholics looked up to him because he represented the Catholic religion in its purest light. He was also respected for his vehement critique of the conservatism of the Catholic Church during the same period.

He advocated for the use of condoms and supported LGBT rights. He opposed the need for forced chastity for priests.

He was in the spotlight for a long time, yet he disliked the inherent popularity of his position.

He withdrew from public view for a while, spending time in semi-retreat. However, when he came back into the public eye in the middle of the 1980s and spoke on topics like homelessness, his message once again found broad and popular acceptance.

It seems that many were still aware of his original message from the 1950s. Abbe Pierre also became a vocal opponent of J. Marie Le Pen's nationalist viewpoint. Abbe Pierre disagreed that immigrants were to blame for all of France's problems.

He advocated for immigrants to the very end of his life, particularly regarding housing.

Abbe Pierre was embroiled in controversy for his support of his old friend Roger Garaudy, despite his history of rescuing Jews from the Nazis during World War II and his fervent opposition to the extreme right in France.

According to Roger's book, Israel overstated the scope of the Holocaust and exploited it as justification for mistreating the Palestinians.

He really and fervently believed in the equality of men, therefore despite this incident, his reputation was usually untarnished.

He was consistently chosen as France's most likable guy in the years leading up to his death. He specifically requested to not be nominated to make room for "someone from the younger generation." The North African immigrant and football player Zinedine Zidane succeeded him.

In particular, he was a spokesperson of the Catholic Church who was able to appeal to even those who were anti-Catholic. His death brought France together in paying tribute to a remarkable figure who brought together many opposed elements.

He advocated for the values of helping others and upholding the Christian tenet of "doing unto others as you would have them do unto you."

Introduction

He established the Emmaus movement in 1949 to aid the underprivileged, the homeless, and refugees.

Although he was one of the most well-liked people in France, his name eventually disappeared from such surveys.

The fifth of eight children, Grouès (Abbe) was born on August 5, 1912, in Lyon, France, into a well-to-do Catholic family of silk merchants. Héra Mirtel, a writer, was his aunt. He was raised in Irigny, a town close to Lyon.

When he first visited an Order circle a fraternity known as the "Hospitaliers veilleurs," in which the members were mostly from the middle class to help the underprivileged by offering barbering services and met François Chabbey, he was twelve years old.

When Grouès joined the Scouts of France, he earned the moniker "Meditative Beaver" (Castor méditatif).

He decided to enter a monastic order in 1928 when he was 16 years old, but he had to wait until he was 17 and a half years old before he could do so.

Grouès joined the Capuchin Order, the main Franciscan branch, in 1931, renounced his inheritances, and donated all of his holdings to charitable organizations.

Brother Philippe, also known as frère Philippe, spent seven years as a resident of the Crest monastery. After suffering from serious lung illnesses that made it impossible for him to handle the demanding and austere monastic life, he was forced to depart in 1939.

He was appointed chaplain of the La Mure hospital in the Isère department, followed by the Côte-Saint-André orphanage.

He received his ordination as a Roman Catholic priest on August 24, 1938, and barely a few months before Poland was invaded, in April 1939, he was appointed curate of Grenoble's cathedral.

On the day of his priestly ordination, Jesuit Fr. Henri de Lubac advised him to "ask the Holy Spirit to give you the same anti-clericalism as the saints."

He was enlisted as a non-commissioned officer in the railroad transport corps when World War II began in 1939. His official biography states that during the Rafle du Vel' d'Hiv mass arrests in Paris in July 1942 and another raid in the non-occupied zone near Grenoble, he assisted Jews in fleeing Nazi persecution: "Two escaping Jews enlisted his assistance in July 1942.

He went right away to get instructions on how to produce fake passports after learning that persecution was occurring. In August 1942, he

began assisting Jews in traveling to Switzerland
"

His use of a pseudonym stems from his involvement with the French Resistance during World War II when he went by various aliases. Based in Grenoble, a significant Resistance hub, he assisted Jews and other politically persecuted individuals in fleeing to Switzerland.

He helped Jacques de Gaulle, Charles de Gaulle's brother, and his wife flee to Switzerland in 1942.

In the Vercors Plateau and the Chartreuse Mountains, he helped create an area of the maquis where he was recognized as one of the local authorities.

By establishing Grenoble the first sanctuary for STO resistance fighters, he assisted individuals in avoiding being drafted into the Nazi forced labor program that was agreed upon with Pierre Laval.

He also launched the covert publication L'Union patriotique indépendante. In 1943, Lucie Coutaz, a member of the Resistance who subsequently served as his secretary and his aide in his charitable work until she died in 1982, temporarily provided him with sanctuary.

He was detained twice, the first time in 1944 by Nazi police in the Pyrénées-Atlantiques city of Cambo-Les-Bains.

However, he was swiftly freed, and he continued to Spain and Gibraltar before enlisting in General de Gaulle's Free French Forces in Algeria.

He joined the French Navy as a chaplain aboard the battleship Jean Bart at Casablanca during the Free North Africa movement.He had developed into a significant figure and a representation of the French Resistance.

He received the Médaille de la Résistance and the Croix de guerre 1939–1945 with bronze palms at the conclusion of the war.

His experience would shape him for the rest of his life, teaching him the need of dedicating himself to defending basic human rights using legal methods and, if necessary, through a type of civil disobedience theory.

Early Childhood & Life

He was the fifth of eight children and was born Henri Marie Joseph Groués on August 5, 1912, in Lyon, France, to a well-to-do Catholic family. His father was a successful silk dealer with a keen sense of justice.

Henri, who had a spiritual bent from an early age, wanted to become a missionary when he was just 12 years old.

He first learned the importance of helping the needy when he went with his father to an Order circle, the fraternity of the "Hospitaliers veilleurs."

When he was 16 years old, he opted to enter a monastic order after realizing his true destiny. He was, however, forced to put off achieving this goal for a while since, at the age of 16, he was seen as being too young.

He eventually joined the Capuchin Order in 1931, the main branch of the Franciscan convent Notre Dame du Bon Secours in St. Etienne.

He donated all of his worldly things to charity and renounced all of his money and inheritances. He changed his name to Brother Philippe as a result of leaving behind his previous identity as Henri Marie Joseph Grouès.

Session 2

The French magazine Emmaüs debuted in 1949. Its name is a nod to an Israelite hamlet mentioned in the Gospel of Luke when two followers welcomed Jesus after his resurrection but failed to recognize him.

In this approach, Emmaus' goal is to aid the underprivileged and homeless. It is a nonreligious institution. The first Emmaus Companions community was founded in Neuilly-Plaisance, France, not far from Paris, in 1950.

The Emmaus neighborhood sells discarded items to make money for the building of homes. "In a way, Emmaus, it's similar to the wheelbarrow, shovels, and pickaxes appearing before the flags. a kind of societal fuel produced by rescuing victorious folks."

Since it was initially difficult to get money, Abbé Pierre decided to compete on the Radio Luxembourg game show Quitte ou double (Double or Nothing) in 1952. He won 256,000 francs in the end.

During the very harsh winter of 1954 in France, when the homeless were passing away on the streets, Abbé Pierre rose to fame.

In response to the rejection of the proposed lodging legislation, he made a memorable statement on Radio Luxembourg on February 1, 1954, and requested that a conservative publication read by "the powerful" publicize his call:

Come aid, my pals, At 3 a.m. tonight, while holding the eviction notice that had rendered her homeless the day before, a lady died of exposure while lying on the pavement of Sebastopol Boulevard.

More than 2,000 people put up with the cold each night while going without food, without bread, and more than one is almost naked. Emergency housing is insufficient to deal with this nightmare.

Hear me out: in the last three hours, two help centers have been established, one in Courbevoie and the other under canvas at the foot of the Pantheon on Montagne Sainte-Geneviève Street. We must open them everywhere since they are already overflowing. Tonight, we must hang out signs under a light in the dark at the entrances of locations that provide blankets, bunks, and soup.

These placards should read, under the heading "Fraternal Aid Center," the following straightforward message: "If you suffer, whoever you are, enter, eat, sleep, recover hope, here you are loved."

A month of severe frosts is predicted. All of humanity must have the same desire to prevent this scenario from occurring for as long as the winter persists and as long as the centers are in operation and their brothers are living in abject poverty. Let's love one another enough to act on it right now, I beg of you. Let us get a magnificent gift from all of our suffering: the French national spirit. I'm grateful.

The homeless may get assistance from everyone. We want 5,000 blankets, 300 large American tents, and 200 catalytic burners by tonight or, ideally, tomorrow. Bring them right away to the Hotel Rochester, 92 La Boetie Street.

At eleven o'clock tonight, in front of the tent on Montagne Sainte-Geneviève, volunteers and vehicles to transport them should congregate. Thanks to you, no man, no kid, will spend the night in Paris sleeping on the streets or by the river.

I'm grateful.

The next day, the press reported on an "uprising of kindness" (insurrection de la bonté), and the now-famous appeal for aid resulted in the collection of 500 million francs in contributions (Charlie Chaplin contributed 2 million).

This massive quantity overburdened telephone operators and the mail service, and it took weeks to organize, distribute, and locate storage space for the gifts around the nation due to their sheer bulk.

Additionally, this call for assistance drew volunteers from all across the nation, including affluent bourgeois who were moved by the Abbé's appeal to first carry out the redistribution and then replicate the initiative throughout France.

Abbé Pierre had to set up his movement swiftly, thus on 23 March 1954 he founded the Emmaus communities.

Volunteers in an Emmaus community provide housing, a place to eat, and a place to work for those who are homeless. Many Emmaus volunteers, from various age groups, religious and ethnic backgrounds, and social backgrounds, were once homeless themselves.

Abbé Pierre made an effort to demonstrate to those in need that they, too, could serve others and that the weak could still assist the weaker.

"Abbé Pierre and the Ragpickers of Emmaus," a novel by Boris Simon that detailed the suffering of impoverished ragpicker communities, contributed to the public's understanding of the Emmaus neighborhood.

Abbé Pierre presented the English version of the book to President Eisenhower in the oval office in 1955.

The communities of Emmaus swiftly grew throughout the globe. A Sunni (Muslim), a Melkite (Catholic) archbishop, and a Maronite (Christian) writer created the first multiconfessional Emmaus group in Beyrouth

(Beirut, Lebanon) in 1959, with the help of the Abbé.

The political career of Abbe

Abbé Pierre was elected deputy for the Meurthe-et-Moselle department in both National Constituent Assemblies in 1945 and 1946 as an independent close to the Popular Republican Movement (MRP), which was primarily composed of Christian democratic members of the Resistance, on the recommendation of de Gaulle's entourage and with the approval of the archbishop of Paris.

He was re-elected to the National Assembly in 1946, but this time as an MRP member. In 1947, Abbé Pierre was elected vice president of the World Federalist Movement, a global federalist organization.

Abbé Pierre decided to abandon his MRP membership on April 28, 1950, after a violent accident in Breast that killed a blue-collar worker named Édouard Mazé.

In a letter titled "Pourquoi Je quitte le MRP " ("Why I Quit the MRP "), he criticized the political and social stance of the MRP party. He later joined the Marc Sangnier-founded Ligue de la Jeune République, a Christian socialist organization, but ultimately decided to abandon his political career.

Before his term was over in 1951, he went back to doing what he loved to do best: helping the homeless. He bought a dilapidated home in the affluent Neuilly-Plaisance neighborhood in Paris with the few indemnities he got as a delegate.

The priest started to fix the roof and the whole home, which astounded his neighbors and eventually used it to build the first Emmaüs base (because, according to him, it was simply too big for one person).

The Abbé eventually ended his engagement in representative politics, choosing instead to devote his time and energy to the Emmaus charitable organization, although he never totally left politics behind, taking strong positions on a wide range of issues.

So, in 1956, when the global decolonization movement was just getting started, he made an effort to persuade Tunisia's leader Habib Bourguiba to achieve independence without resorting to force.

He met Colombian priest Camilo Torres (1929–1966), a forerunner of Liberation theology, at several international conferences at the end of the 1950s.

Torres sought his counsel over the Colombian Church's critique of "workers' priests." In 1955 and 1956, he also met Mohammed V of Morocco and US President Eisenhower.

He spent several months in 1962 living at Charles de Foucauld's hideaway at Béni-Abbés (Algeria). [Reference required]

The Abbé was then invited to India by Jayaprakash Narayan in 1971 to speak on behalf of France and the Ligue des droits de l'homme (Human Rights League) about refugee-related problems.

After receiving an invitation from Indira Gandhi to address the issue of Bengali refugees, the Abbé established Emmaus communities in Bangladesh.

Positions of Abbe Pierre in the church

The Abbé's views on the Church and the Vatican also sparked debate. His social ideas and activities were sometimes overtly socialist and antagonistic to the Church.

He kept up a friendship with the liberal French Catholic Bishop Jacques Gaillot, to whom he remembered his responsibility of "instinct of a calibrated insolence." He didn't like Mother Teresa.

Despite her efforts on behalf of the underprivileged, Abbé Pierre did not appreciate her rigid commitment to Catholic moral doctrine.

He did not get along well with the Vatican. In 2007, L'Osservatore Romano, a publication not renowned for covering priest deaths, took some time to report on his passing.

Pope Benedict XVI received harsh criticism from Abbé Pierre's followers for not making an exception even though it is not normal for the Pope to express sorrow on the passing of certain priests.

While Benedict XVI did note his passing in private audiences, the Vatican's spokesperson, Father Lombardi, directed the media to the French Church's statement. In two interviews with French cardinals Roger Etchegaray and Paul Poupard, the Church provided official responses.

Although he earned a lot of attention for what he saw to be the extravagant lifestyle of the Vatican (particularly when he criticized John Paul II for his costly trips), the people did not take well to his remarks.

Tarcisio Bertone, the Cardinal Secretary of State, praised his "activity on behalf of the poor": "Upon learning of Abbe Pierre's passing, the Holy Father expresses gratitude for his work on behalf of the least fortunate, which served as a testament to Christ's kind nature.

He begs the Lord to accept him into the tranquility of His kingdom, entrusting to divine compassion this priest whose whole life had been devoted to combating poverty.

His Holiness gives you a deep papal blessing of consolation and hope, which he extends to the bereaved family, to members of the Emmaus communities, and everyone attending the burial."

He disagreed with Christian tradition, church authorities, and a sizable number of French Catholics who adhered to the traditional teachings of the Church because he supported married clergy and the ordination of women.

According to British state media, it was these same positions that helped him win over France's dwindling left-wing Catholic population.

Did he acknowledge having had casual intercourse with women in his 2005 book Mon Dieu... Pourquoi? (God... Why?), which he co-wrote with Frédéric Lenoir.

This was a breach of his solemn vow of chastity. Abbé Pierre disregarded people's worries that same-sex adoption robs children of a mother or father and transforms them into objects, despite extremely vocal objections from the general public to the practice.

The Abbé also disagreed with the Catholic tradition's stance.

International acclaim

For many years, Abbé Pierre had the distinction of being named France's most popular person; however, in 2003, Zinedine Zidane overtook him and moved into second place.

In a televised vote to determine Le Plus Grand Français, Abbé Pierre placed in third place in 2005. (The Greatest Frenchman).

He was appointed Grand Officer of the National Order of Quebec in 1998, and Jacques Chirac presented him with the Grand Cross of the Legion of Honor in 2004.

Additionally, in 1991, he was awarded the Balzan Prize for Humanity, Peace, and Brotherhood among Peoples. "for having battled his whole life to uphold democracy, human rights, and peace.

For having fully committed himself to assist in the alleviation of both spiritual and bodily pain.

For having sparked unwavering support for the Emmaus Communities regardless of one's race, religion, or nation."

Accidents and medical conditions

He suffered from many illnesses, especially lung ailments while he was young. He avoided harm in several risky scenarios:

He was on a journey to India in 1950 when his aircraft had to make an emergency landing because one of the engines had failed.

His boat capsized in the Rio de la Plata in 1963, halfway between Argentina and Uruguay. While 80 people perished around him, he managed to stay alive by holding on to a wooden portion of the boat.

He later displayed the pocket knife that had allowed him to live on a trip to Algiers. He was very appreciative of the youngsters living in an orphanage, and he requested Léon-Etienne Duval, the cardinal archbishop of Algiers, to assist the institution (or Kasbah).

Together, these incidents shaped the perception of Abbé Pierre as a miracle worker.

Abbe Pierre Death

Abbé Pierre was still active up to his death on January 22, 2007, from a lung infection, at the Val-de-Grâce military hospital in Paris. He was 94 years old.

He supported illegal immigrants, helped the homeless (the "Enfants de Don Quichotte" campaign, which took place at the end of 2006 and the beginning of 2007), and supported social groups that advocated occupying vacant homes and businesses (squats), among other causes.

La Croix, the Christian social daily newspaper, was still something he read every day. After the Enfants de Don Quichotte NGO mobilized, President Jacques Chirac advocated changes to the legislation on housing for the homeless.

He went to the National Assembly to oppose these MPs. Despite his doubts about the legislation's actual worth and application, Abbé Pierre's name was eventually given to the bill by

Minister of Social Cohesion Jean-Louis Borloo (UMP).

He had fought against conservative deputies in 2005 who tried to amend the Gayssot Act on housing projects (loi SRU), which intended to impose a 20 percent housing project cap in each municipality under threat of penalties.

After being honored by dignitaries, several hundred regular Parisians visited the Val-de-Grâce chapel to view Abbé Pierre's body, including professor Albert Jacquard, who fought with Abbé for the cause of homelessness.

President Jacques Chirac, former President Valéry Giscard d'Estaing, Prime Minister Dominique de Villepin, numerous French Ministers, and of course the Companions of Emmaus, who were seated at the front of the congregation in the cathedral per Abbé Pierre's final wishes, attended his funeral on January 26, 2007, at the Cathedral of Notre Dame de Paris.

He was laid to rest at a cemetery in Estherville, a tiny town in Seine-Maritime. The Lyon archbishop, Cardinal Philippe Barbarin, hinted at potential beatification, although it doesn't appear likely to happen anytime soon.